SURROUNDED BY SEA

GAIL GIBBONS

Life on a New England Fishing Island

Holiday House / New York

For Donna and Charlie Rogers

Printed and bound in September 2023 at Toppan Leefung, DongGuan City, China
www.holidayhouse.com
5 7 9 10 8 6 4
This book was originally published
by Little, Brown & Co. in 1991.

Library of Congress Cataloging-in-Publication Data
Gibbons, Gail.
Surrounded by sea : life on a New England fishing island /
by Gail Gibbons.
p. cm.
ISBN 0-8234-1941-X (hardcover)
ISBN 0-8234-2021-3 (paperback)
1. Atlantic Coast (Me.)—Social life and customs—Juvenile literature.
2. Fishing villages—Maine—Atlantic Coast—Juvenile literature.
3. Islands—Maine—Atlantic Coast—Juvenile literature.
4. Fishing—Maine—Atlantic Coast—Juvenile literature. I. Title.
F27.A75G53 2005
974.1—dc22
2004054089

ISBN-13: 978-0-8234-1941-8   ISBN-13: 978-0-8234-2021-6 (pbk)
ISBN-10: 0-8234-1941-X   ISBN-10: 0-8234-2021-3 (pbk)

The ferry rests at the end of the wharf. It brings supplies and passengers from the mainland to the fishing village. Most of the passengers are island people who spent the winter on the mainland and are ready to return home.

The greeters onshore are island folk who stayed on through the winter. Now it's the beginning of a new season. The daffodils are blooming and the tulips are up.

It's spring on the fishing island. Different kinds of boats bob about in the harbor waters.

Along the shore, near the general store, some fishermen have beached their boats. There they scrape and clean barnacles and algae off the bottoms of their boats. Some boats get a fresh coat of paint.

Against the harbor shoreline are workshops built on pilings nestled among the rocks. Empty lobster traps are piled on the wharves.

buoy

Inside one of the workshops a lobsterman gets ready to set his traps. First he overhauls his traps by fixing the older ones. The older traps are wooden. The newer traps are made of plastic-coated wire. He cuts lengths of rope, called warps, to connect buoys to the traps.

This lobsterman paints his buoys red and white. Each lobster fisherman or fisherwoman uses his or her own colors to identify the buoys. The lobsterman sets out early the next morning before the sun is up and when the seas are calm. His lobster boat, stacked high with empty traps, leaves the harbor.

sternman

His boat bobs on the waves along with the other lobster boats. He works with his partner, called a sternman, and drops the traps overboard one by one. The sternman is working at the back, or stern, of the boat while the lobsterman steers the lobster boat. Each day they will bring more traps out to sea until all the traps are finally set. Then the lobstermen are ready for a new season.

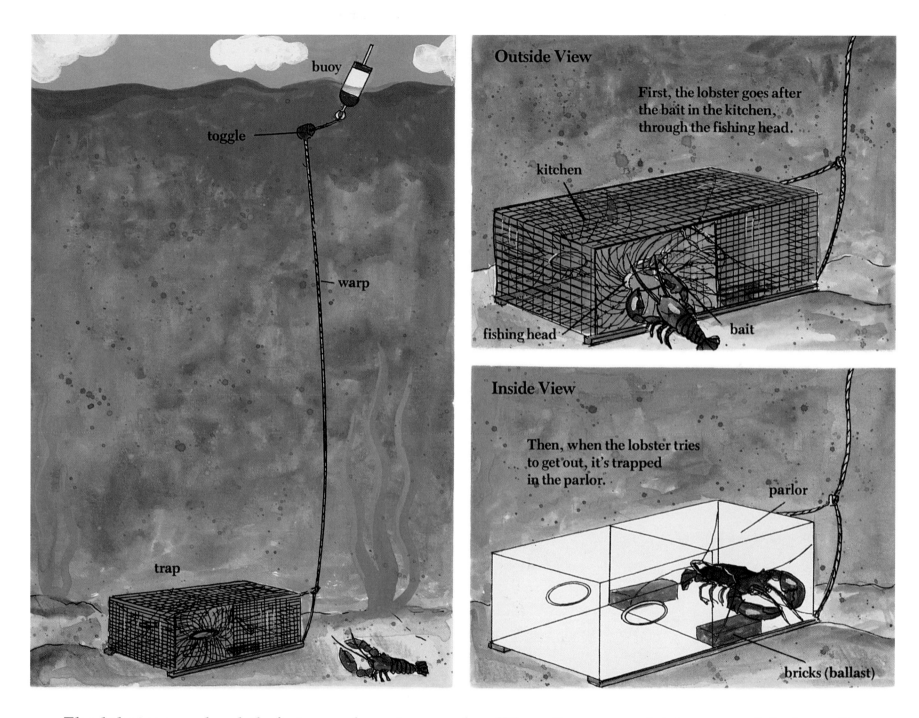

The lobstermen haul their traps almost every day. When they are catching more lobsters, they haul more often. This is how a lobster trap works.

Above the island, a small plane is approaching the gravel runway. It's the mail plane! Bags of mail are delivered to the post office in the general store. The storekeeper on this island is also the postmaster. While the islanders wait for their mail to be sorted, they chat about the weather and island news.

All around the island, vegetable and flower gardens are planted. Along the shore, islanders dig
for clams and hunt for mussels during low tide.

It's summer on the fishing island. Now what a busy place the island is. There are more people. A small ferry brings summer people and more supplies. It goes back and forth to the mainland more often than the big ferry does.

An island caretaker gets one of the summer cottages ready for a group of people who come to spend the summer on this beautiful, remote island.

Everyone on the island comes to the Fourth of July lobsterbake. There's a big party on the beach that lasts all day. It ends with fireworks over the water at night.

Twice a week in the summertime, the Farmer's Market is open. Island people bring fresh vegetables from their gardens to sell. There are baskets of berries that grow wild on the island. Freshly baked pies and cakes are for sale, too. There are handicrafts made by the islanders, and one island boy sells his painted seashells.

A red hot-dog truck is parked on one of the wharves. Islanders and summer people stop by to pick up food and snacks to eat in the warm sunshine. Children play along the shoreline. They wave to the people in the boats offshore.

One of the lobstermen hauls up a trap and pulls out a lobster. He measures its size to make sure it's not too short or too long. Lobsters that are too small or too big are thrown back into the sea. This one is just the right size. The fisherman puts bands on its claws so it won't pinch him or any of the other lobsters he catches. He drops it in a bin filled with other lobsters.

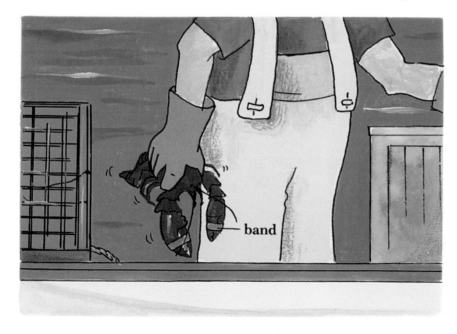

band

The sternman puts a fresh bag of bait into the trap and drops the trap overboard again. At the end of the day they will sell their lobsters to a lobster buyer who, in turn, will sell them to stores and restaurants on the mainland.

It's fall on the fishing island. It's quieter along the harbor shore. The summer people have all gone home. Summer cottages and homes are shut down by the island caretakers. Only the people who live on the fishing island remain. The small island ferry that went back and forth during the summer has stopped its trips. Now the big ferry goes back and forth to the mainland about once a month.

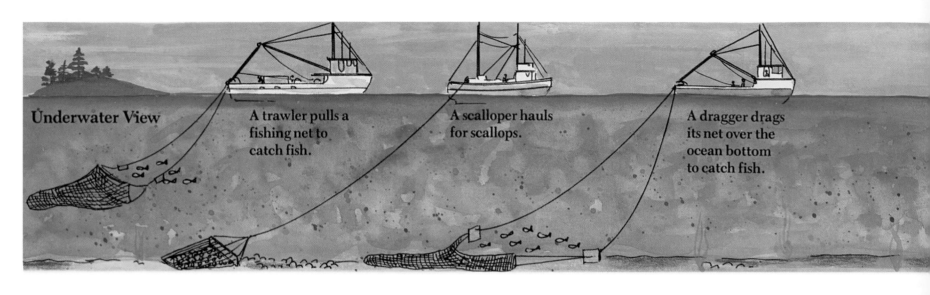

Underwater View

A trawler pulls a fishing net to catch fish.

A scalloper hauls for scallops.

A dragger drags its net over the ocean bottom to catch fish.

dory

motorboat

dinghy

But the fishermen are still busy.

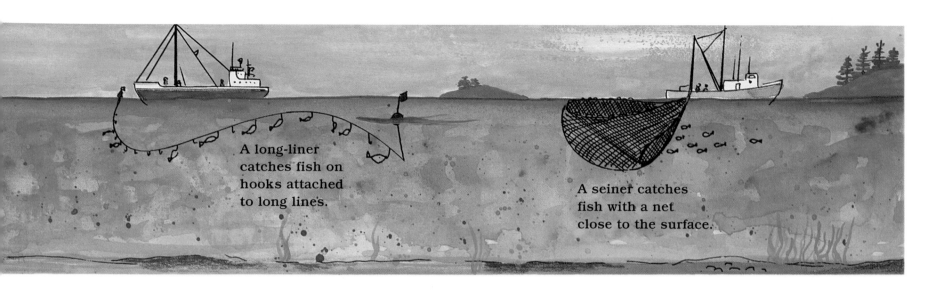

A long-liner catches fish on hooks attached to long lines.

A seiner catches fish with a net close to the surface.

lobster boat

All kinds of fishing boats move along the horizon.

The island children go back to their one-room schoolhouse, where their teacher greets them. At the town hall, the small library remains busy. Some of the island people harvest their gardens. Other island folk take boats to nearby islands to pick cranberries. Over near the church, a few islanders spruce up the fire engine.

Off in the distance looms a huge tanker making its way toward an inland river. The captain needs assistance to navigate through the waters. One of the lobster boats is also a pilot boat. It brings the pilot, someone who knows this part of the ocean, out to the tanker to help guide it into port.

It's winter on the fishing island. It is very quiet. Some of the fishermen and their families have gone to the mainland to get away from the cold, harsh winter. Now, only the hardy souls remain. Snow falls to the ground. After school, children make snow sculptures and skate on the ice pond.

During the cold nights, lights glow from island windows. The beam from the lighthouse shines in the distance. The island has its own generator-run power company. A microwave tower on the island picks up and sends phone signals to and from the island so the residents can make calls.

Some lobstermen still haul their traps on clear days. Otherwise, they work inside their warm shops mending traps. Inside their homes, folks make handicrafts to sell at the Farmer's Market next summer.

The people that stay behind love their island home. There they will stay through the winter. Soon spring will return to the fishing village out at sea, and once again the island will be a busy place.